Mysterious Places

Peter Hepplewhite ✛ Neil Tonge

Publisher: Zuza Vrbova
Editor: Richard Widdows
Art Editor: Donna Payne
Designer: Michele Ashby
Illustrations: Mike Foster, Stephen Capsey and Carl Venton
at Maltings Partnership
Picture Researcher: Suzanne Williams
Production: Christine Campbell
Cover design: Ian Butterworth

Consultant: Philip Mantle of the British UFO Research Association

Picture Credits

Jean-Loup Charmet: page 34;
Hulton Getty Images: page 9;
Images Colour Library/Douglass Baglin: page 19;
The Kobal Collection: pages 16-17;
Photodisc Inc.: cover, top
Pictures of Record Inc.: pages 22 and 25;
Gerald Ponting/Fortean Picture Library: cover, bottom;
Rex Features: page 35;
Telegraph Colour Library: page 36 (Rick England), page 43.

Published in 1997 by Hamlyn Children's Books, an imprint of Reed International Books,
Michelin House, 81 Fulham Road, London SW3 6RB and Auckland and Melbourne
Illustrations © 1997 Reed International Books Limited
Text © 1997 Peter Hepplewhite & Neil Tonge.
The authors have asserted their moral rights.
ISBN 0 600 59298 7
First Edition
10 9 8 7 6 5 4 3 2 1
A CIP catalogue record for this book is available from the British Library.
Printed in Italy by Olivotto

Contents

CURSE OF THE PHARAOHS The discovery of the treasure trove tomb of the pharaoh Tutankhamun in 1922 was hailed across the world as a great triumph. Yet many people connected with the adventure soon died in weird ways. Was it just coincidence — or were they all victims of an ancient Egyptian curse?

DREAMTIME In Australia, at the turn of the 20th century, four schoolgirls and their teacher vanished into thin air during a Valentine's Day picnic at a sacred Aboriginal site. Only one of them was found. Some people think that the others entered a spiritual "dreamtime" beyond our world — and have never returned.

THE EARTH SERPENT A strange mound lies in the American state of Ohio, shaped like a giant snake. It once contained curious Indian artefacts from all over North America — but it could well have been a good deal more than a burial place for Native tribal chiefs.

GIANTS OF STONE On Easter Island, hundreds of huge stone figures stare out across the Pacific Ocean, like guardians of an ancient landlocked secret. We try to find out who carved these staggering statues — and why.

THE SACRED CIRCLE The magical site of Stonehenge has held an endless fascination for millions of visitors. Yet its function remains a mystery. Was it a place of ancient human sacrifice, or a gigantic observatory that traced the movement of the stars?

Introducing more great titles in
The Unexplained series.

When it comes to the world of the supernatural and the paranormal, there's a lot to talk about. Together with *Mysterious Places*, these are the other brilliant books in this brand new series hot off the Hamlyn production line.

THE UNCANNY ❯ ❯

Funny goings-on in mind, body and spirit

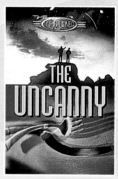

❮ ❮ ALIEN ENCOUNTERS

Close connections of the extra-terrestrial kind

HAUNTINGS ❯ ❯

Spooky travels through time and space

Mysterious Places

Have you ever visited a place where you felt a chill run down your spine? All over the world, baffling events have unfolded in places that are haunted by spirits and powers far beyond our understanding. Many of these sites have been considered sacred for generations — and disturbing them can release the strangest forces.

Mysterious Places describes five such locations in four different continents, and looks at the intriguing theories that have been put forward to explain them.

When you read about uncanny events like these, you need to start with an open mind. Nonsense or common sense?

The Unexplained series lets YOU decide what to believe...

CURSE OF THE PHARAOHS

 power cut plunged the city of Cairo into darkness, and

LORD CARNARVON **DIED IN AGONY**

In a plush Egyptian hotel, the wealthy aristocrat had lost his fight for life. Several thousand kilometres away in England, his favourite pet terrier Susie howled for hours —before dropping down dead.

Lord Carnarvon had spent a small fortune financing the archaeologist Howard Carter's long search for the tomb of Tutankhamun, in Egypt's Valley of the Kings. A hot, forbidding place, the valley had been chosen by many pharaohs as their last, undisturbed resting place. Inside this burial chamber a threatening inscription read:

DATE:

5 April 1923

TIME:

1:55 a.m.

PLACE:

Cairo, Egypt

"Death will slay with his wings whoever disturbs the peace of the pharaoh."

T he curse was intended to warn away **tomb-robbers**, but it didn't stop the ambitious Englishmen. They were determined to take out the treasures.

Perhaps Carnarvon should have heeded a famous mystic of the time, who had sent him a warning telegram the day before the sealed tomb was opened. Later he was bitten by a mosquito. The bite became infected when he cut it shaving, and he was rushed to Cairo...

"Do not enter the tomb stop
Disobey at your peril stop
If ignored will suffer sickness stop
Not recover stop
Death will claim you in Egypt stop"

COUNT HAMON

Lord Carnarvon's death attracted worldwide attention from the newspapers. Fact after fact emerged to support the theory that he was a victim of the ancient curse.

One of the more incredible facts came to light when the mummified body of the pharaoh was examined seven months later in November 1923. A small cut was found on the left cheek... precisely the same place where the fateful mosquito had bitten Lord Carnarvon.

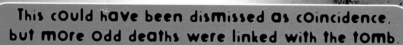

This could have been dismissed as coincidence, but more odd deaths were linked with the tomb.

GEORGES BÉNÉDITE, the French historian, died as a result of a fall, just after seeing the burial chamber.

● **GEORGE GOULD**, a rich American friend of Lord Carnarvon, died of pneumonia shortly after visiting the tomb of Tutankhamun.

● **ARCHIBALD REID**, who had used X-rays to examine the Tutankhamun mummy, complained of exhaustion. He was sent home and died soon afterwards.

● **RICHARD BETHEL**, Carnarvon's secretary in Egypt, was found dead of heart failure some time after the discovery of the tomb.

9

RICHARD BETHEL

6 **6**

Six years after the discovery of the tomb, 12 of those who had been present at the opening of the sealed chamber in 1923 [above] were dead. A year later, only two of the original excavators were still alive.

12 **12** **12**

Strangely enough, the archaeologist

CARTER DIED OF NATURAL CAUSES

in 1939, after living a long and active life.

DEATH BY ATOMIC RADIATION?

The mysterious deaths of so many people involved in the excavation of Tutankhamun's tomb have yet to be explained. One of the strangest suggestions was put forward by the atomic scientist Louis Bulgarini in 1949. He believed that: "It is definitely possible that the ancient Egyptians lined the floors with uranium. Rock containing gold and uranium was mined in Egypt. Such radiation could kill a person."

However, Dr Derry, who had examined the body of Tutankhamun, was 88 when he died. This was not a man killed-off in the prime of his life! Investigators have demonstrated that many of the "victims" had no connection with the tomb at all.

ANCIENT CURSES?

The pharaohs' tombs were "protected" by magic spells, which were meant to frighten off robbers and enemies of the pharaohs — but not to kill them. Yet ...

Do not

In 1966 Egypt's Director of Antiquities, Mohammed Ibrahim, begged that Tutankhamun's treasures were not sent to an exhibition in Paris. He had been suffering terrifying nightmares in which he died a terrible death.

let the

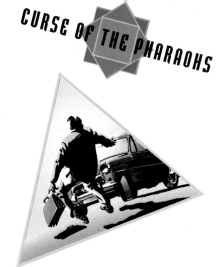

At a final meeting Egyptian government officials refused to stop the exhibition leaving Cairo.

Afterwards Ibrahim stepped out into the bright sunshine, but failed to see the car hurtling towards him. His death was instantaneous . . .

HAD TUTANKHAMUN'S CURSE CLAIMED ANOTHER VICTIM? **11**

treasure

THE CURSE MOVES ON...

Dr Gamal Mehrez took over as Director of Antiquities after Mohammed Ibrahim's death, and he made fun of the stories of the curse.

leave the

Yet after a busy day supervising the packing of the treasures, ready for transport to an exhibition in London, he died in his sleep — the very same night.

country!

Doubting the Curse!

ne of the last surviving members of Howard Carter's expedition, Richard Adamson, spoke out many times against the curse, with shocking consequences. After an early outburst at stories of the curse, his wife died suddenly. In 1969, stories of the curse hit the newspapers again: 24 hours after Adamson spoke out against them, Adamson's son broke his back in a plane crash. Undaunted, Adamson appeared on television, claiming the curse to be nonsense. On leaving the television studios, the taxi in which he was travelling crashed. Adamson was thrown from the taxi, and a swerving car only just missed his head. Finally, he conceded:

> "Until now I refused to believe that my family's misfortunes had anything to do with the curse. But now I'm not so sure."

THE CURSE
TAKES FLIGHT

Even the flight crew who took Tutankhamun's treasures from Cairo to London seemed dogged by misfortune. Flight-Lieutenant Rick Laurie died in 1976 of a heart attack. Ken Parkinson, the Flight-Engineer, suffered a heart attack the following year — at the same hour as the flight that had brought the collection to England. Before their mission to Egypt, neither man had any heart problems.

Ψ

The mystery remains. Was the spirit of Tutankhamun reaching beyond the grave to claim its victims? Or did those who experienced such bad luck find an explanation for so many coincidences?

DREAMTIME

The heat was fierce and the ground was parched and arid. A horse and carriage sped along, leaving behind it clouds of dust from the rough track. Ahead of it, a vast rock loomed out of the flat landscape like an upturned boat. Here and there along the rock rose jagged peaks, and narrow crevice-like wrinkles scarred its surface. The rock appeared as if it came from another planet — dusty red during the day, but turning to burning colours of yellow, gold and scarlet in the light of the setting sun.

DATE:

14 February 1900
(St. Valentine's Day)

PLACE:

Hanging Rock,
South Australia

Aborigines, the native Australians, had long respected this site as a place where spirits lived. Their presence could be felt in the breezes that stirred little columns of dust and whispered in the branches of the trees. To "Europeans" the weathering of the rocks looked as though boulders had been piled in layers, giving the impression that the rocks were "hanging" in the air...

SO

THEY

CALLED

IT

HANGING

ROCK.

In the carriage a party of excited schoolgirls were going on a picnic. A driver and two female teachers accompanied them — quite enough adults to look after them and keep them out of harm's way.

Having eaten their picnic, some of the girls lay back in the welcome shade of the few trees to escape the hot afternoon sun. But four of them became bored, and set off to explore the curious rock. One of their schoolmistresses left a little later — possibly to check on the safety of her pupils. Several hours later the rest of the group woke to find their friends were missing, and they soon became anxious.

NO TRACE OF THE OTHERS

A big search was organised, but their companions couldn't be seen. The rest of the party were about to leave to seek help when they heard a hysterical cry — and the youngest of the missing girls rushed out of the bush. She was so terrified that she was unable to speak. And there was no sign of the three others or their mistress.

E xtensive searches were carried out for a week — until one of the girls was suddenly found on the rock. She had a few cuts and bruises on her hands and face ... but her bare feet were unmarked. She could remember nothing of her absent days, as if she had fallen into a strange dream ...

17

WAS EVER FOUND. . .

Theory 1: Fiction...

The story was written by the Australian writer Joan Lindsay, and later made into a film called *Picnic at Hanging Rock* (1975). Hanging Rock resembles many strange rock formations in Australia, which Aborigines believe to be the sacred site of spirits.

Joan Lindsay would not admit that the story was entirely made up. At the beginning of her novel she explains in a note: "Whether *Picnic at Hanging Rock* is fact or fiction, my readers must decide for themselves. As the fateful picnic took place in 1900, and all the characters who appear in this book are long since dead, it hardly seems important."
After writing it, she changed it to read: "Fact or fiction or both?" The new words were never included, but they heighten the mystery. *Picnic at Hanging Rock* remains remarkable in the fact that it is the only one of Joan Lindsay's books that refers to a set date. Another unusual fact about Joan Lindsay is that she never wore a watch — because watches stopped not only on her, but also on people around her.

Theory 2: Or fact?

Aborigines of Australia believe that there was a time when every living thing existed in a spirit world, called "Dreamtime". The world was created and our life on Earth began, but when things died they returned to Dreamtime. Aborigines contact this spirit world in dreams and they believe that the physical body can disappear into it. In Dreamtime the spirit roams freely over the landscape. In this state it is possible to pass messages over long distances, and there has been evidence of this happening.

19

Could the missing schoolgirls still be trapped in "Dreamtime"?

The Dingo Killer

In the early 1980s another strange Australian story made big news...

A young Christian couple, the Chamberlains, went on a camping holiday at Ayers Rock in the heart of the desert — the most sacred of all Aborigine sites. As they sat round the fire with other campers, they both heard a weird scuffling noise. Mrs Chamberlain ran to the tent to check that her nine-week old baby girl was safe.

BUT THE LITTLE COT WAS EMPTY...

A search was organised but only shreds of blood-stained baby clothing were found. Mr and Mrs Chamberlain were distraught, and they sought comfort in their strong religious beliefs. They thought that a wild dog, or dingo, must have carried their child off. Many reckoned differently, and accused them of killing their baby as some sort of sacrifice. A court case followed, and the couple were judged to be innocent. But doubts lingered on...

Aboriginal Curse

Near Tennant Creek, in the Australian outback, a number of curious stone boulders rest on the skyline like giant marbles. According to Aboriginal legend, the spirits placed the rocks there at the "Dawn of Time". In 1980 one of the boulders was removed to a nearby National Park. Mick Taylor, the leader of the local Aborigines, was outraged and he warned, "Our people are [now] cursed ... sickness and death will follow." Within months several Aboriginal children fell ill — and one year later, Mick Taylor himself suddenly died of meningitis.

21

THE EARTH SERPENT

Walter Pidgeon could hardly believe his eyes. A Hopewell Indian called De-coo-dah had told him stories of strange wonders on the land — and now he had taken him to see one. He would not be disappointed.

The historian climbed to the top of a small hill for a better view. From there he could see what looked like a mound of earth, but as he looked more carefully he began to make out the shape of a raised serpent, twisting and turning on the ground. Also in view were other unusually shaped mounds, one of which appeared as a giant eagle skewered to the ground. Pidgeon returned to the Indian, who stood somewhat ill at ease.

"What do you know about these earthen shapes, De-coo-dah? They are so strange."

He took out his notebook and licked the end of his pencil, ready to write. But De-coo-dah could offer little more explanation.

The Native American reckoned that they may have been placed there by the Great Spirit who had created the Earth. Or perhaps they had been built by a race of people long since gone from this land. "They are a form of writing in the Earth," he explained.

Walter wrote down every word eagerly. Then he began to sketch the outline of the mounds from the top of a nearby hill.

"Are there more?"

he asked De-coo-dah, his excitement growing every second. "Yes, many more," was the Indian's reply...

DATE:

1840

PLACE:

Ohio,
United States of
America

Walter realised that he had been led to a mystery from the distant past.

Walter Pidgeon set himself the mission of recording and measuring every mound he could find. His notebooks were soon bulging with sketches and notes. It was just as well, for the local farmers were not as respectful. Many of the mounds disappeared under their ploughs, and so we only have Pidgeon's sketches as evidence of their appearance.

SACRED SERPENT

The largest and the most confusing of the shaped mounds in Ohio is the Great Serpent. Its coils stretch for nearly 400 metres, and it is 1.5 metres high. Because there is no evidence of burials and no objects have been found, it can't be dated accurately. A 19th-century church minister claimed that it was the original site of the Garden of Eden — and that this was the snake that had tempted Adam and Eve. One modern invesigator has argued that it isn't a serpent at all: it's in fact built in the shape of the constellation of stars known as the **LITTLE DIPPER.**

The Hopewells were not the only Native Americans to leave behind strange features on the ground. Weird and wonderful sites are found all across the United States:

COPPER CROSS

This copper ornament (left) comes from Moundville, Alabama. A centre of 3,000 people, it had over 20 mounds around the year 1200 AD.

POVERTY POINT MYSTERY

At Poverty Point in Louisiana there are six spectacular octagons, each inside the other. It has been estimated that it would have taken 20 million baskets of earth to build — an enormous project. But nobody knows who it was built for, or how the people who built it had such a good knowledge of geometry.

GIANT EAGLE OF STONE

Thousands of rocks form the shape of an eagle in Georgia. Its wingspan measures

37M

Constructed around 1,500 years ago, its purpose remains a mystery.

WHO ? BUILT ? THE ? MOUNDS

THE UNEXPLAINED

Archaeologists believe that the mounds were built by at least three different Native American cultures. The earliest dated back to the year 2000 BC.

The most famous of these, the Hopewells, appeared about 200 AD. They put treasures of copper and mica, sometimes gold and silver, in the tombs of their chiefs. These were also used as sites for ceremonies.

The Hopewells were great traders, and many burial items came from far away. Historians have found bird talons from the Appalachian Mountains and sharks' teeth from the Gulf of Mexico.

THE EARTH SERPENT

A later Indian society, the Mississippians, erected huge mounds from about 700 AD. Many of them looked like pyramids without tops. They were probably influenced by the architecture of the Aztecs in Mexico.

On some of the mounds, archaeologists have found the remains of wooden post-holes. This may mean that the tops of some mounds had been the sites of wooden temples.

ERE THEY BURIAL MOUNDS, EREMONIAL SITES, OR MAPS F THE SUN AND THE STARS?

Further west, in the Bighorn Mountains, huge wheels were marked out in stone. Archaeologists think they perhaps plotted the position of the Sun throughout the year. But no definite proof exists for their use ...

DATE CHART

2000 BC
The first Native American culture begins in the Mississippi Valley.

200 AD
The Hopewell Indians begin building mounds in the hills of Ohio.

700 AD
The Mississippians start to build their huge earthworks.

1840
Walter Pidgeon begins his research of the mounds in Ohio.

1858
Walter Pidgeon publishes his book *Traditions of De-Coo-Dah*. This describes and explains the mounds. De-Coo-Dah was a medicine man who gave Pidgeon his original information about the mounds.

20th century
Archaeologists reveal information about the sites and the many interesting objects that are found there.

Sinister mounds

Many people who have visited the Ohio mounds experience a strange, creeping coldness sweep over their bodies.

One of the oddest incidents happened to Robert Harner, a Harvard professor. He recalled an Autumn visit to the mounds. As he stopped to stare at them, dead leaves began to rise up – and soon surrounded him in a column.

(Not a breath of wind was to be felt that day.)

Harner was overcome with a terrible feeling of evil which made his skin creep. He turned and fled from the place, sensing all the time that something was at his heels. Daring to turn round, he noticed that the leaves had settled back on the ground as if they had never been disturbed.

GIANTS OF STONE

DATE:

Easter Day 1722

PLACE:

Easter Island,
Pacific Ocean

Admiral Roggeveen of the Dutch East India Company steered his cargo ship towards a hilly island in the southern Pacific Ocean. This was a place where no European had been before. The crew had been at sea for many weeks and were keen to go ashore to enjoy some exercise and to eat fresh food.

Once ashore, many of them began to feel a sense of unease. Scattered around the island, they were amazed to find hundreds of huge stone statues looming over them. They cast large black shadows in the setting sun. On all the islands they had visited, these men had seen nothing like this. Most of the statues were on the slopes, facing out to sea. These hollow-eyed, long-eared sentries stared out across the island to the distant horizon, as if expecting a special visitor . . .

All of the figures had been quarried from an extinct volcano at the centre of the island.

HOW WAS THIS POSSIBLE, USING ONLY STONE TOOLS?

Even more amazing, they had been hauled long distances and then pushed into an upright position. Some of the 600 figures stood almost 16 kilometres from the quarry and weighed over 30 tonnes, with the heaviest estimated to weigh a staggering 80 tonnes.

To have achieved such a task would have required a huge workforce, strong ropes and wooden rollers. Yet the people of the island lived in scattered groups and had only simple stone tools. Even more mysterious were the abandoned tools scattered around the quarry site — a long extinct volcano. It was as if the people had suddenly dropped their stone tools one day, never to return.

onuments

Admiral Roggeveen was determined to find an answer to the riddle. He approached one of the islanders and, with the help of an interpreter, asked: **"WHO BUILT THE STATUES?"** The islander's eyes hardened as he stared at the Admiral. It was pointless to ask further questions. After several days roaming the island looking for possible clues, the Admiral loaded his ship with fresh supplies and sailed away. He left behind him the mystery of the stone giants that the local people called *moai*.

carved?

How were the statues erected?

In the late 1970s archaeologists tried to lift the statues by using some of the tools available to the islanders. They found that stone hammers were capable of gouging out the shape of the statues. Rubbing stones could smooth and polish the surface. One of the small statues was even dragged along using ropes, and levered into position. Two long poles were placed at the edge of the statue and then gradually levered into an upright position. But no attempt was made to raise larger statues — and how this was done remains a fascinating mystery.

Who were the Long Ears?

According to the many islanders who finally agreed to talk, the statues had been set up by a people whom they called "Long Ears". They were the chiefs of the island and had made their ears grow longer by attaching weights to them. The Long Ears ruled over the rest of the population, who were "Short Ears". As their masters, they forced the Short Ears to work building the statues. Eventually the Short Ears could bear it no longer and rebelled against the Long Ears. A terrible war followed in about 1700 AD, with women and children killed as well as warriors. But the Short Ears outnumbered the Long Ears and finally won. The victory of the Short Ears heralded the end for the great stone giants. No more were ever built.

ccording to anthropologists, the Short Ears are similar to other Pacific islanders, while the Long Ears resemble early South American people. It has been suggested that the Long Ears may have sailed to Easter Island from South America. But if this is true, why did they settle only on Easter Island? Other experts think that the Long Ears were Pacific islanders who developed their own culture.

Date Chart

ABOUT 400 AD	The first people arrive and settle on Easter Island
ABOUT 1100 AD	The first large statues are set up
ABOUT 1700 AD	Statue building comes to a sudden end — perhaps because of a war between the "Long Ears" and the "Short Ears"
1722 AD	Admiral Roggeveen is the first European to land on the island
1782 AD	French sailors under Admiral La Pérouse topple several figures (above) and take one colossal stone head back to a Paris museum
19th CENTURY	The first scientific investigations of the statues take place

Some Europeans found it hard to understand how people with a primitive technology could have erected such impressive monuments. Among the most absurd suggestions are the ideas of Erich von Daniken, who is convinced that the Earth has experienced a number of visits by creatures from outer space. These creatures provided all the technology that was necessary to raise the statues!

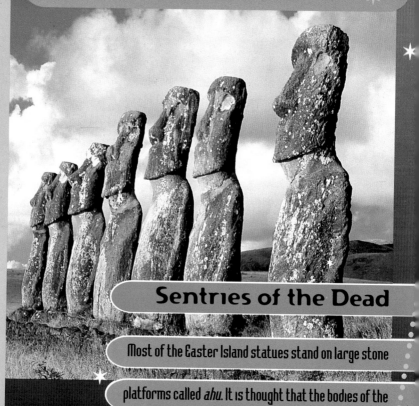

Sentries of the Dead

Most of the Easter Island statues stand on large stone

platforms called *ahu*. It is thought that the bodies of the

dead were placed here for the birds and weather to strip

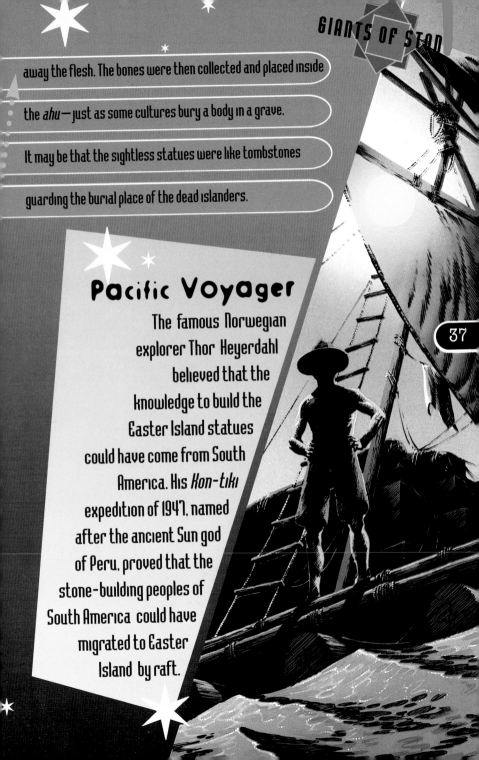

away the flesh. The bones were then collected and placed inside

the *ahu*—just as some cultures bury a body in a grave.

It may be that the sightless statues were like tombstones

guarding the burial place of the dead islanders.

Pacific Voyager

The famous Norwegian explorer Thor Heyerdahl believed that the knowledge to build the Easter Island statues could have come from South America. His *Kon-tiki* expedition of 1947, named after the ancient Sun god of Peru, proved that the stone-building peoples of South America could have migrated to Easter Island by raft.

THE SACRED CIRCLE

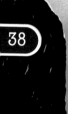

In the early morning light a crowd of people, many of them modern Druids in long white robes, start to walk along the narrow pathway between two earth banks that run up the slope from the north-east. Three men lead the group. One man, with a great blanket of a beard and a large talisman round his neck, walks slightly ahead of his two companions. These two men carry banners with mystical signs painted on them.

DATE:
21 June

TIME:
Dawn

PLACE:
Stonehenge,
Southern England

The sky begins to look like metalled
silver as the Sun's light creeps over the
rim of the horizon. The three leaders pass
through the outer stone circle and move
silently into the centre. There, three huge
upright stones cast giant shadows across the
ground. Not a word passes between the remainder
of the group as they form a circle facing towards
the east. Soon a great spear of sunlight breaks
through the circle of stones and strikes the leader.
His face glows, as if in a furnace. At that moment two
members of the group press their lips to rams' horns.
The sound of the horns blast out a greeting to the new day —
and the height of Summer. A look of pleasure sweeps across
the crowd and they close their eyes, saying a silent Druid
prayer for the precious gifts of light and warmth.

Who built STONEHENGE?

There are nearly 900 stone circles sites in Britain, and thousands more stretch across Western Europe. But Stonehenge is the most famous of them. Until the 18th century it was thought that Stonehenge had been built by the Druids — priests of the Celtic people. Now, archaeologists have proved that it was abandoned for at least a century before the Druids appeared in England.

Approximate Date Chart

3100 - 2200 BC   Stonehenge I is built by Stone Age peoples. It consists of a basic ditch and earthen bank, which later form the outer circle. But around 2600 BC the site is abandoned and becomes scrubland.

2100 BC   Stonehenge II is erected, using about 80 bluestones that come from the Preseli Mountains of South Wales, 385 kilometres away. Like the later and bigger sarsen (sandstone) stones, they were probably pulled along wooden rollers by teams of men and oxen. These stones formed concentric circles in the centre of the site, though the circles were never completed. The Heel Stone is erected: when you stand in the centre of Stonehenge at midsummer (the Summer Solstice), the Sun rises precisely over its tip.

II

III

Ancient monuments such as Stonehenge are called "megaliths". The word comes from the Greek *megas* (large) and *lithos* (stone).

2000 BC Stonehenge III begins. The bluestones are removed, and in their place appears a sarsen circle of 30 uprights, with continuous lintels. Inside this is a "horseshoe" shape of sarsen stones round the Altar Stone. The nearest source of sarsen sandstone was 30 kilometres away, yet some of these uprights weighed 45 tonnes.

At some stage, 20 of the bluestones were set within the sarsen horseshoe.

1550 BC The 60 remaining bluestones are placed between the horseshoe and the circle. Now complete, Stonehenge has become the most impressive Bronze Age monument in northern Europe.

The site probably fell into disuse around 1000 BC— although nobody knows why. It was another thousand years before the Romans invaded Britain

WHAT WAS STONEHENGE USED FOR ?

Theory 1: A Guide to the Stars?

In 1934 a professor from Glasgow was sailing his boat off the Isle of Lewis in Scotland, heading home after a day's relaxation. Silhouetted against the full Moon stood the standing stones of Callanish *(below)*. Curious, he sailed to shore and climbed up the slope to stand in the centre of the stone circle. Looking up, he noticed that the monument was in line with the guiding Pole Star.

After his discovery, the professor began a quest around hundreds of stone circle sites throughout Britain. By very careful measurements, he became convinced that all the stone circles were in line with the rising and setting of the Moon and the Sun. Other scholars added to the growing evidence. Gerald Hawkins, Professor of Astronomy at Boston University in the USA, claimed that Stonehenge *(right)* was like a colossal computer: the stones were placed in positions that mapped out the positions of the Sun, Moon and stars.

42

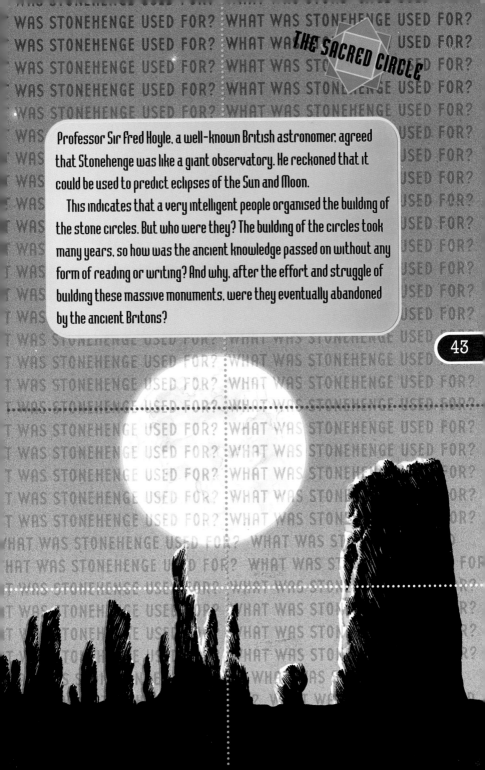

THE SACRED CIRCLE

Professor Sir Fred Hoyle, a well-known British astronomer, agreed that Stonehenge was like a giant observatory. He reckoned that it could be used to predict eclipses of the Sun and Moon.

This indicates that a very intelligent people organised the building of the stone circles. But who were they? The building of the circles took many years, so how was the ancient knowledge passed on without any form of reading or writing? And why, after the effort and struggle of building these massive monuments, were they eventually abandoned by the ancient Britons?

43

Theory 2: Lines of Magic Power

In 1920 an amateur historian, Alfred Watkins, suggested that the ancient stone circles and earthworks were connected by trackways. When looked at on a map they seemed to be in the same positions as the stars. This led Watkins to the conclusion that all the monuments were in fact an ancient "star map" plotted all over southern England.

The pathways connecting the sites seemed to stretch for hundreds of kilometres. Watkins became convinced that these "lines" (or "leys" as he called them), had magical properties. They had been built so that nothing could stand in the way of the hidden energy that buzzed along them. Walking along them meant people could become charged with spiritual energy, almost like a battery.

So powerful are these energy fields that students of this ancient wisdom believe the stones themselves could be powered to fly through the sky. This sounds fantastic, but there have been legends recalling ancient British flying machines. The most famous of these stories is of a Druid called Bladud. According to legend, he flew on one of the giant stones but crashed and was killed. And the secret of "energising" the stones was lost with his death.

44

Theory 3: Alien Landing Zone

There are those who find it difficult to understand that early people had the intelligence or organisation to construct such a huge monument. They believe that if these places are "observatories", then aliens from outer space must have visited Earth and built structures like Stonehenge. They argue that, because of its size, Stonehenge could have been used as a beacon to guide incoming spaceships from distant planets.

CURSE OF THE PHARAOHS

antiquities valuable objects from distant history

archaeologist person who digs up buildings and objects connected with people who have lived in the ancient past

aristocrat titled member of the wealthy classes

excavators people (or machines) who dig up the ground

mosquito insect that in hot countries carries the disease malaria, which can be fatal

mummified the ancient Egyptians preserved their pharaohs' bodies with chemicals before wrapping them in cloth as "mummies"

mystic person who claims direct contact with divine forces

pharaohs powerful kings of the ancient Egyptians

radiation dangerous loss of energy from a source without physical contact

Tutankhamun pharaoh "boy king" of Egypt from 1361 to 1352 BC; 12 years old when he gained the throne and only 21 when he died, he is famous only because of the discovery of his magnificent tomb at Thebes

undaunted not discouraged (not put off)

uranium most common radioactive metal in the Earth's crust

DREAMTIME

Aborigines local ("Native") black Australians

companion friend, often on trips and journeys

crevice deep opening in rock

dingo now native wild dog of Australia, originally taken there by the Aborigines

distraught overcome with grief and worry

Dreamtime Aboriginal name for the beginning of time, in which there were many strange spirits and magical creatures

hysterical uncontrolled, panic-stricken

meningitis dangerous infection that inflames the brain

novel fictional storybook for adults

weathering action of weather's elements on the landscape, especially on rocks

THE EARTH SERPENT

archaeologist person who digs up buildings and objects connected with people who lived in the ancient past

Aztecs civilisation of Mexico in the 12th to 16th centuries, noted for their pyramid-shaped buildings

ceremonies the official parts of events like weddings and seasonal celebrations

constellation group of stars

forming figures in the night sky
geometry area of mathematics dealing with figures and shapes
Hopewells native American Indians of the Ohio area, also known as Hopewellians
legend fantastic story that is based mainly or totally on myth
octagon eight-sided figure
serpent large snake, often mythical rather than real
talons claws of a bird of prey

 ## GIANTS OF STONE

admiral high-ranking naval officer in charge of a fleet of ships
anthropologist person who studies societies, especially those from the past
archaeologist person who digs up buildings and objects connected with people who lived in the ancient past
Dutch East India Company organisation of merchants based in Holland which transported valuable goods by ship from the Dutch colonies
extinct dead forever, when referring to animal species and volcanoes
primitive not developed, especially when applied to peoples or societies
sentries soldiers on guard or watch

 ## THE SACRED CIRCLE

astronomer scientist who studies the stars
concentric parallel, when applied to curves and circles rather than straight lines
Druids priests of the pre-Christian religions of ancient Britain; they still exist
eclipse total or partial disappearance of the Sun or the Moon from view
energise to give energy or active strength to an object
furnace large oven for smelting coal and metals
oxen cow-like beasts of burden and ploughing, used throughout ancient cultures
scrubland uncultivated land covered with wild grass, bushes and small trees
silhouette solid black outline of an object
Summer Solstice midsummer; the longest day in the northern hemisphere
talisman object, usually carved or inscribed, believed to protect the owner or wearer from evil influences

Index